Contents

Text Formatting

Getting started

You will probably already be familiar with some of the more basic features of Microsoft Word by the time you come to use this book.

This chapter will remind you how much you know and you may learn a few useful new tips.

Project: Create an advertising leaflet

You are going to follow the steps given below to create a leaflet advertising a day out in London. The finished leaflet will look something like Figure 1.1 opposite.

Tip:
If you are using Word 2002 or 2003 and the task pane opens, close it by clicking its close icon (x).

Entering and formatting text

In a new Word document type the words East of England Railways. Press Enter.

Highlight the text and click the Center button. Make the text Times New Roman, 24pt.

Make the text Italic using the button on the Formatting toolbar.

Now add a shaded box around the heading. On the menu bar click Format, Borders and Shading and click the Borders tab.

▶ Click on Box style and in the Apply to section select Paragraph. Click OK.

▶ With the text still highlighted, select Format, Borders and Shading from the menu bar and then click the Shading tab.

▶ Choose a fairly dark shade and in the Apply to section select Paragraph. Click OK.

▶ With the text still highlighted, change the colour of the text to white using the Font Color button on the Formatting toolbar. —————

▶ Click in the line below the box. (You may need to double-click if you forgot to press Enter after the heading.) Change the font colour back to black.

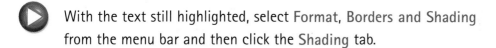

East of England Railways

Summertime Offers!

We are offering all our customers an exciting day out in London at a very special price. Relax in First Class while you speed into the capital, enjoying our complimentary refreshments en route.
With your travelcard you can

- ✓ Cruise on the Thames aboard a motorised launch
- ✓ Savour a complimentary meal with wine included
- ✓ Visit the London Eye, marvelling at the fantastic views over the capital
- ✓ Choose one of the following activities in the afternoon:
   - o do some shopping in Knightsbridge or Regent Street
   - o visit the stupendous Tate Modern Art Gallery
   - o visit the new galleries at the Science Museum
- ✓ Return home in First Class luxury and comfort.

You have a choice of weekday departure dates and times:

Departure Dates and Times
1. 08.00, 09.00 or 09.40 from Norwich
2. 08.40, 09.40 or 10.15 from Ipswich
3. 0900, 10.00 or 10.30 from Colchester

You may return on any train except those leaving Liverpool Street between 17.00 and 18.30 Monday to Friday.

London ✱ Colchester ✱ Ipswich ✱ Norwich

Figure 1.1

▶ Insert a blank line by pressing Enter and then type in the heading Summertime Offers! Press Enter again.

▶ Highlight this heading and click the Bold and Center buttons on the ————— **B**
Formatting toolbar. The text should be 24 point, Times New Roman – or you can choose a different font.

▶ Leave a blank line and type the first block of text as shown in Figure 1.1, making it left aligned, 12pt.

Creating the bulleted list

▶ Insert a blank line and then type in the list of 8 things you can do with your travel card. (Don't worry about the ticks, circles or indenting yet.) Press Enter twice.

▶ Highlight the list and convert it into a bulleted list by clicking the Bullets button on the Formatting toolbar.

▶ Now you can change the standard bullet symbol into a ✔. From the menu bar select Format, Bullets and Numbering.

▶ With the Bullet tab selected, click on Customize.

A dialogue box appears:

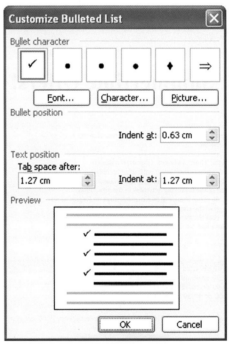

Figure 1.2: Changing the style of bullet

Tip:

If the correct symbol does not appear click on **Character** (**Bullet** in 2000) and select a symbol. The ✔ symbol is under the **CommonBullets** or **Wingdings2** font option.

▶ Select the tick mark and click OK.

▶ Highlight just the 5th – 7th items in the list and use the Increase Indent button on the Formatting toolbar to indent those items. Their bullet symbol should change but you can also use the dialogue box shown above to select a different symbol.

▶ Use the Bullet Position and Text Position options on the dialogue box to adjust the layout if you like.

▶ Click below the list and type the sentence You have a choice of weekday departure dates and times:

▶ Insert another blank line.

Creating the numbered list

You can create a numbered list by just typing the list without numbers, and letting Word add them for you later.

▶ In Arial 14pt type the heading Departure Dates and Times.

▶ In Arial 12pt type the list of departure dates and times, but don't type the numbers 1, 2 and 3. Press Enter at the end of the list.

▶ Convert it into a numbered list by highlighting the items and clicking the Numbering button on the Formatting toolbar.

▶ Adjust the indent of the list using the Decrease Indent button, so that the numbers are lined up with the heading.

▶ Use the menu item Format, Borders and Shading to draw a border around the heading and list, and then shade in the heading the same way you did earlier.

▶ Insert a blank line after the list and in Times New Roman, 12pt type the sentence You may return... and then press Enter again twice.

Inserting on-line clip art

Microsoft Word is supplied with a small selection of clip art or you might have other CDs with clip art images. If not, there is a plentiful supply available (copyright free) from the Microsoft web site.

▶ Click Insert, Picture and then Clip Art.

▶ At the bottom of the Insert Clip Art task pane click Clip art on Office Online (Clips Online in Word 2000).

🔲	Organize clips...
🔡	Clip art on Office Online
❓	Tips for finding clips

Figure 1.3: Accessing on-line Clip art

Tip:
To insert a blank line in a numbered or bulleted list press **Shift-Enter** on the keyboard.

Tip:
In Word 2000 click **Clips Online** and then **OK** in the Connect to Web dialogue box.

You will be connected directly to the Microsoft Clip Art web site.

Figure 1.4: The Microsoft Office Clip Gallery site

Type Trains in the Search for box and select photos as the media type. Click Go.

Select the image(s) you wish to download and click Download. Click Download Now on the next screen.

The image(s) will be stored in the Downloaded Clips category of your local clip art gallery.

In the task pane enter Trains into the search text box and choose to search in All collections.

Click Go or Search (Word 2000/2002).

Click the image and it will be inserted into your word document.

Size the image by dragging one of the corner handles until you are satisfied with the result.

Centre the image by clicking the Center button on the Formatting toolbar.

Don't forget to disconnect if you are not permanently online!

Tip:

In Word 2000 click the image and then click the **Insert clip** button which appears on a mini-toolbar.

Inserting autoshapes

The last line of the advertising leaflet has place names separated by autoshapes that are inserted from the Drawing toolbar.

▶ Insert two blank lines after the picture and click the Center button.

▶ Type in the four city/town names (London, Colchester, Ipswich, Norwich) each separated by six spaces.

▶ Select AutoShapes, Stars and Banners from the Drawing toolbar. Insert a star (the top right one is a good one) between the names London and Colchester. Adjust its size by dragging a corner handle.

▶ Use the Fill tool on the Drawing toolbar to shade in the star.

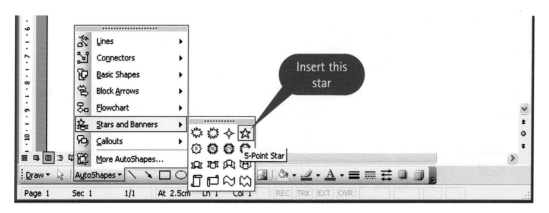

Figure 1.5: Inserting an Autoshape

Now you can copy and paste the star between the other place names. A good way of doing this is to hold down Shift and Ctrl together while you drag the star to as many places as you want it. Holding down Shift keeps all the stars in a straight line, and holding down Ctrl copies, rather than moves, the star.

That's it! You can now save your work and print it – and book your day out...

Tip:

If the drawing canvas is displayed (Word 2002/3) remove it by selecting **Tools**, **Options** and click the **General** tab. De-select the last general option relating to the drawing canvas. Click **OK**.

Tip:

You can use the cursor keys to adjust the position of the star when it is selected.

Chapter 2

Setting Styles

Word allows you to define a style with a particular font, size and format which you can then apply to any text in a document. Look at this page – how many styles can you count? One for the chapter heading, one for the paragraph heading and so on.

If a style is changed, all the text that has been formatted with that style will change automatically. So if the chapter heading style was changed, all the chapter headings would take on the new style. This helps to keep everything consistent.

The Style box

When you create a new document based on the standard Normal template, certain styles will be pre-set for you.

Start Word and open a new blank document if you have not already got one on the screen.

Click on the arrow to the right of the Style box at the left-hand end of the Formatting toolbar.

Tip:

If you are using Word 2002 or 2003, you may find that new styles are created automatically for you, which is confusing.

To avoid this: Select **Tools**, **Options** and click the **Edit** tab. De-select the **keep track of formatting** option.

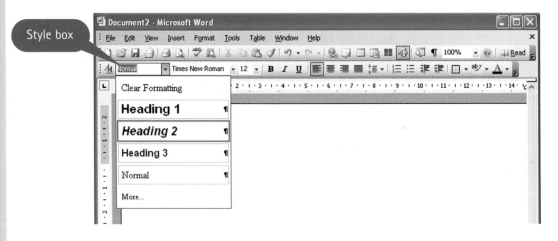

Figure 2.1: The Style box

Project: A theatre programme

You are going to create the outline of a programme for a school production of The Merchant of Venice. The programme will use 4 different styles of text called Head1, Head2, Head3 and Normal.

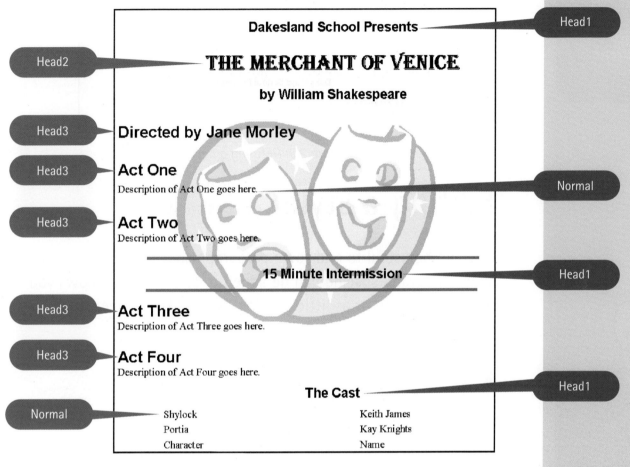

Figure 2.2: The theatre programme

Defining a style

- In the new blank document type the four headings Dakesland School Presents, The Merchant of Venice, by William Shakespeare, Directed by Jane Morley (don't centre them or use any special font.)

- Highlight the heading Dakesland School Presents and manually change the formatting of this text to Arial font, size 12pt, bold and centred.

▶ With the insertion point still in the text, click in the Style box at the left end of the Formatting toolbar.

▶ Type a name for your new style e.g. Head1 and press Enter.

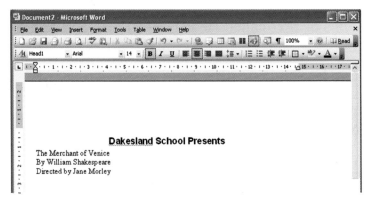

Figure 2.3: Defining a new style

Editing a style

It would be useful to add some paragraph spacing to the Head1 style. Paragraph spacing can be added to any text and allows you to leave as much or as little spacing as you like between paragraphs.

▶ Right-click in the heading (not in the word Dakesland which Word thinks is a spelling mistake) and select Paragraph from the pop-up menu.

▶ In the dialogue box, enter 6 in the Spacing Before box and 3 in the Spacing After box. Click OK.

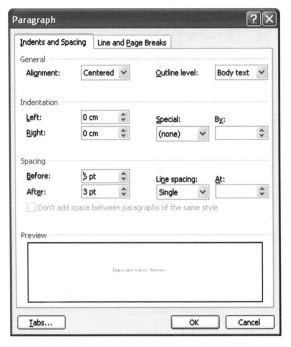

Figure 2.4: Paragraph spacing

Now that we have made manual changes to the format, we can edit the actual style:

▶ Click the Styles and Formatting button.

▶ With the top heading line selected, right-click the style Head1 in the Styles and Formatting task pane.

▶ Select update to Match selection from the drop-down list.

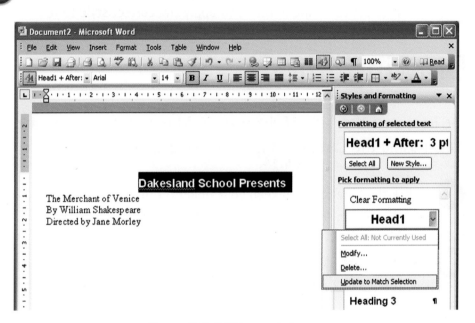

Figure 2.5: Editing a style

Tip:

In Word 2000 select the top heading line, click the arrow beside the style box and click the style **Head1**.

Select the first option shown in the Modify style dialogue box and click **OK**.

Adding more styles

Now you can define two more styles called Head2 and Head3.

Head2 uses 16 point Algerian font, bold and centred. It has paragraph spacing of 12 points before and 3 points after.

Head3 uses 14 point Arial, bold and left justified.

▶ Highlight the second line, The Merchant of Venice.

▶ Follow the same steps as before to create the style Head2.

▶ Highlight the fourth line, Directed by Jane Morley and create style Head3.

Tip:

Look back at Figure 2.2 to make sure you're on track!

Applying styles

▶ You can apply style Head1 to the line by William Shakespeare by highlighting it and selecting Head1 in the Style box.

▶ Type the rest of the programme using the predefined Normal style. When you get to the members of the cast, use the Tab key (to the left of Q on the keyboard) to keep the names neatly lined up.

▶ Then select each line in turn and apply the correct style to it.

Drawing lines

The lines on either side of the text 15 Minute Intermission are drawn using the Line tool on the Drawing toolbar.

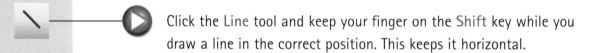

▶ Click the Line tool and keep your finger on the Shift key while you draw a line in the correct position. This keeps it horizontal.

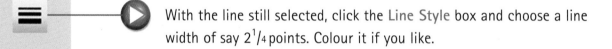

▶ With the line still selected, click the Line Style box and choose a line width of say $2^{1}/_{4}$ points. Colour it if you like.

▶ Hold down the Ctrl key and the Shift key while you drag the line down to create the second line.

---

15 Minute Intermission

Creating a watermark

Watermarks are text or graphics that are printed faintly behind the main body text. You can use a clip art image to make the programme look more exciting!

▶ From the menu select Insert, Picture, Clip Art.

▶ Search for Theatre in All Collections and you should find a suitable picture. Insert the picture into the document.

▶ With the image selected, click the right mouse button and select Format Picture.

▶ Click the Layout tab and select Behind Text, Center alignment. Click OK.

▶ On the Picture toolbar click the Image Control button.

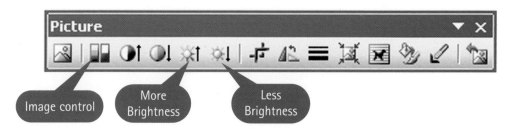

Figure 2.6: The Picture toolbar

Tip:
The Picture toolbar should appear when the picture is selected. If it does not, select **View**, **Toolbars** and click on **Picture**.

▶ Select Washout. (Watermark in Word 2000.)

In Word 2000 you may need to send the picture behind the text again:

▶ Click the right mouse button and select Format Picture.

▶ Click the Layout tab and select Behind Text. Click OK.

You can adjust the brightness of the image by using the More Brightness and Less Brightness buttons on the Picture toolbar.

▶ Save and print your theatre programme.

Chapter 3

Tabs and Tables

Tab

One way of producing neat lists arranged in columns is to set Tab stops and use the Tab key to move between these set positions.

Microsoft Word has default tab positions which appear as faint marks below the ruler underneath the Formatting toolbar.

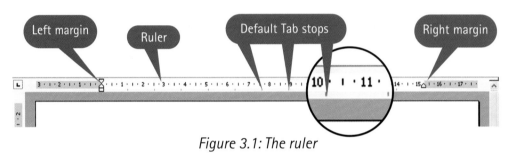

Left margin   Ruler   Default Tab stops   Right margin

Figure 3.1: The ruler

The default tab stops in the screenshot above are 1.27cm apart.

Open a new document.

Look at the ruler line. Are your tabs set the same as in Figure 3.1? They may be slightly different.

To try out the tabs, type the list below using Arial, 14 pt.

Tip:

Don't use the space bar at all. Use the Tab key (to the left of the letter Q on the keyboard) to move between columns. Sometimes you will have to press the Tab key twice or three times.

TEAM LISTS		
Red Team	Green Team	Blue Team
Greg	Rob	Mustapha
Samita	Stephanie	Christine
Carl	Peter	Heidi

You can change the distance between the default tab stops, but it's best to do this before you begin typing, as you are about to find out.

 Select Format on the main menu. Then click Tabs... You will see a dialogue box like the one below.

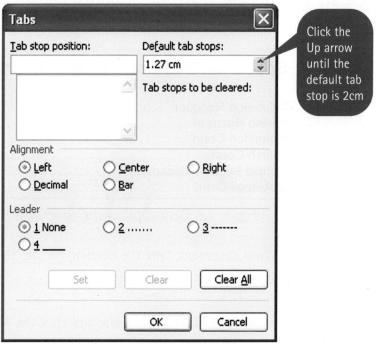

Click the Up arrow until the default tab stop is 2cm

Figure 3.2: Changing default tab stops

 Click the Up arrow in the Default Tab Stops box to set it to 2 cm. Then click OK.

Instant chaos! When the space between the tab stops was smaller, you needed more tab characters between each name. Now these extra characters need to be deleted.

You can either have fun deleting the extra tab stops using the Backspace or Delete key until the teams line up properly again, or you can delete the whole list and start again.

 Save the list as TeamList when you are happy with it, and close the document.

Note:

To the computer, **Tab** is just a character like **A, B, C** and you can delete a tab with the **Backspace** or **Delete** key.

Creating your own style of tabs

You can create your own tab stops wherever you want them – and you can also use leader characters.

These are the dots that make up the dotted line between the items and the prices in the list below:

Sports Centre Price List (per hour)

Badminton Racquet 0.50
Squash Racquet 0.75
Badminton Court 2.50
Squash Court 2.75
Football Pitch (Outdoors) 10.25
Basketball Court 6.00

Figure 3.3: Custom tabs with leader dots

▶ In a new Word document, type the heading for the Sports Centre Price List in Arial, 14pt bold and centred.

▶ Press Enter twice to make a blank line and click the Align Left button on the Formatting toolbar. Change the font to size 12pt and not bold.

▶ Select Format, Tabs.

The dialogue box that you saw before (Figure 3.2) will be displayed.

▶ In the Tab Stop Position box type 3 and click Set.

▶ In the Tab Stop Position box type 12.

▶ Click on Decimal alignment.

▶ Click on Leader option 2.

▶ Click Set and then click OK.

▶ Press the Tab key to begin the list, entering the items separated by Tab and pressing Enter at the end of each line.

Does your price list look like the one above? If so, congratulations, save it as PriceList and close it. Maybe you can think of other times when tabs would come in handy.

Tip:
Never use spaces to try and line things up in columns - always use Tabs - they're brilliant!

Working with tables

Another way of arranging information in neat columns is to insert a table into your document.

Project: Create a weekly school timetable

In this example you learn how to insert a table into a document and type out a timetable something like the one shown below.

Timetable for Term 1				B. Grainger	
	Monday	Tuesday	Wednesday	Thursday	Friday
8.30-9.15	Maths	English	English	Maths	Science
9.15-10.00	English	Maths	English	French	Science
10.00-10.45	P.E.	Maths	I.T.	French	History
10.45-11.15	ASS./BREAK				
11.15-11.45	History	French	Drama	English	Swimming
11.45-12.30	History	French	Science	English	Maths
12.30-1.30	LUNCH BREAK				
1.30-2.15	I.T.	Science	Maths	P.S.H.C.E.	Design & Tech
2.15-3.00	Geography	Science	Geography	Art	Design & Tech
3.00-3.45	R.E.	Games	Geography	Art	English

Figure 3.4

 Start by opening a new document.

 Set the page to landscape orientation by selecting File, Page Setup and clicking Landscape.

Note that you can also change the size of the page margins (the white spaces to the top, bottom, left and right of a page) from the Page Setup dialogue box. We will leave the default settings.

 Type a large, bold heading, for example Timetable for Term 1 and your name

 Press Enter twice and change the font back to Times New Roman, 12pt, left aligned, not bold.

Tip:
A page in **Landscape** orientation is short and wide unlike this page which is in **Portrait** orientation i.e. tall and narrow.

Inserting a table

▶ From the main menu select Table, Insert, Table. You will see a dialogue box like the one below.

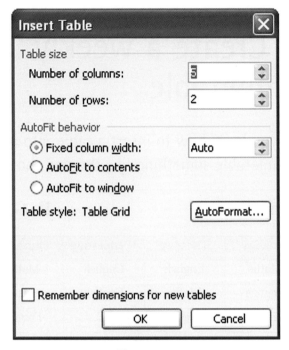

Figure 3.5

▶ Type 6 as the number of columns (or use the arrows).

▶ Press the Tab key to move to the next box, and enter 11.

▶ Leave the Column width as Auto and click the OK button.

A table will be inserted into your document, like this:

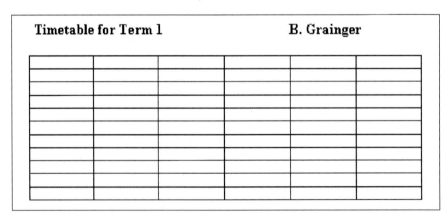

Figure 3.6: An empty table

The cursor should be flashing in the first cell of the table, in the top left-hand corner.

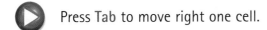 Press **Tab** to move right one cell.

 Type **Monday** and then tab to the next cell.

▶ Type **Tuesday**, **Wednesday**, etc in the cells across the top row.

▶ Press **Tab** when you have typed **Friday** to go to the first cell of the second row.

▶ Now fill in the rest of the timetable so that it looks like the one below. (You can put different subjects and times if you like. It is not necessary to type the whole timetable for this exercise.)

Tip:
Word realises what you're up to and shows **Monday** as a tool tip! Press **Enter** to fill in the rest of the word.

Timetable for Term 1				B. Grainger	
	Monday	Tuesday	Wednesday	Thursday	Friday
8.30-9.15	Maths	English	English	Maths	Science
9.15-10.00	English	Maths	English	French	Science
10.00-10.45	P.E.	Maths	I.T.	French	History
10.45-11.15	ASS./BREAK				
11.15-11.45	History	French	Drama	English	Swimming
11.45-12.30	History	French	Science	English	Maths
12.30-1.30	LUNCH BREAK				
1.30-2.15	I.T.	Science	Maths	P.S.H.C.E.	Design & Tech
2.15-3.00	Geography	Science	Geography	Art	Design & Tech
3.00-3.45	R.E.	Games	Geography	Art	English

Figure 3.7

Changing the height of the cells

The timetable looks rather cramped. It needs to be spread out more.

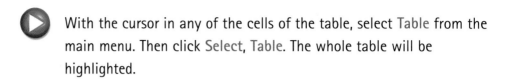 With the cursor in any of the cells of the table, select Table from the main menu. Then click Select, Table. The whole table will be highlighted.

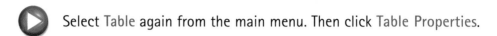 Select Table again from the main menu. Then click Table Properties.

A dialogue box will appear.

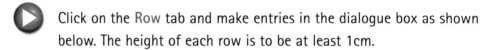 Click on the Row tab and make entries in the dialogue box as shown below. The height of each row is to be at least 1cm.

Figure 3.8: The Table Properties dialogue box

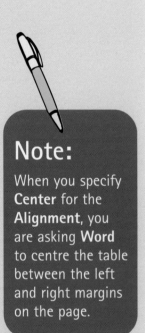
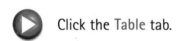 Click the Table tab.

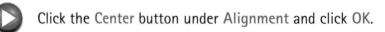 Click the Center button under Alignment and click OK.

Merging cells in a table

Assembly or Break is always at 10.45 on this timetable, and Lunch is always at 12.30. We can spread the words Ass./Break and Lunch Break across several cells.

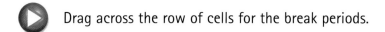 Drag across the row of cells for the break periods.

From the main menu select Table. Then select Merge Cells.

Click the Center and Bold buttons on the Formatting toolbar. You can make the font bigger too.

Now do the same for Lunch Break.

Formatting text in cells

Click the mouse in the cell containing Monday and drag across and down to the bottom right corner of the table to select the cells.

Press the Center button on the Formatting toolbar.

Click in the left margin beside the top row to select it. Click the Bold button on the Formatting toolbar.

You can try a new way of selecting a column – position the cursor just over the top line of the column until it changes to a downward-pointing arrow. Then click.

Select all the cells in the first column. Make them bold too.

Shading

You can shade any of the cells in the table.

▶ Click in the left margin beside the top row to select it.

▶ From the menu select Format. Then click Borders and Shading.

▶ In the dialogue box that appears, click the Shading tab.

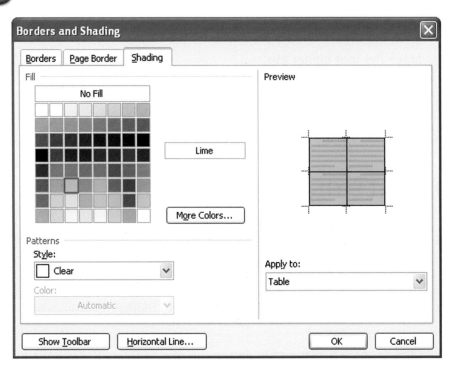

Figure 3.9

▶ Click a colour for the shading, and then click OK.

	Monday	Tuesday	Wednesday	Thursday	Friday
Timetable for Term 1				**B. Grainger**	
8.30–9.15	Maths	English	English	Maths	Science
9.15–10.00	English	Maths	English	French	Science
10.00–10.45	P.E.	Maths	I.T.	French	History
10.45–11.15	**ASS./BREAK**				
11.15–11.45	History	French	Drama	English	Swimming
11.45–12.30	History	French	Science	English	Maths
12.30–1.30	**LUNCH BREAK**				
1.30–2.15	I.T.	Science	Maths	P.S.H.C.E.	Design & Tech
2.15–3.00	Geography	Science	Geography	Art	Design & Tech
3.00–3.45	R.E.	Games	Geography	Art	English

Figure 3.10: The timetable so far

22

Inserting and deleting rows

Suppose you wanted to insert an extra row just before the row for 10.45–11.15 (ASS./BREAK).

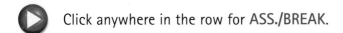 Click anywhere in the row for ASS./BREAK.

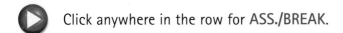 From the main menu select Table, Insert, Rows Above.

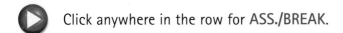 To delete the extra row, select Table, Delete, Rows.

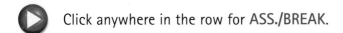 To insert an extra row at the end of a table, click in the very last cell and press the Tab key. (You can delete this row again!)

Changing column widths

To change a column width, put the pointer over one of the boundary lines separating the cells. When the pointer changes to a double-headed arrow, you can drag the boundary line either way to make a column wider or narrower.

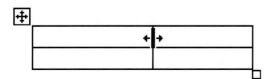

Centering text vertically

You have already centred the text horizontally so that it appears in the middle of a column. You can also centre vertically so that text is right in the middle of the cell.

Centred horizontally	Centred both ways

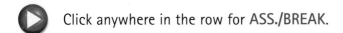 From the menu select Table, Select, Table.

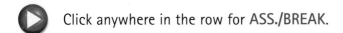 Right-click and hover over Cell Alignment.

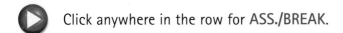 Choose the centre option, Align Center.

It looks great! Save and print your timetable.

Chapter 4

Headers and Footers

Headers and footers are used in printed documents with the header printed in the top margin and the footer printed in the bottom margin.

You sometimes want something to appear on every page of a document – for example a page number, the date, a company logo, the document's title or file name, or the author's name. That's what headers and footers are for.

Project: Create a header and footer for Chess Club stationery

Imagine you are the secretary of the school chess club. You need stationery that you can use for sending letters to members, printing newsletters and producing regular printed bulletins informing members of match dates.

You are going to create the letter shown opposite.

12 April 2005

Mr John Browning
Chess Club Secretary
Middleton High School
Range Barns
Suffolk
RB61 6NM

Dear John

Please find attached a schedule detailing the next round of matches in the East of England Schools Chess Championship.

This is being sent to all High Schools in East Anglia who are members of the East Of England Junior Chess League.

Please let me know if there are any matches that your school will be unable to attend and I will ask the committee if they can be re-scheduled.

Best wishes

Jess Greenwood
Secretary
East Of England Junior Chess League

Enc.

Dakesland High School, Dakes Road, Dakesland, Suffolk DK99 8UI

Figure 4.1: The completed letter

Opening the Header box

First you must open the header and footer area of the Word document.

 In a new Word document select View, Header and Footer. The following header box and toolbar will appear:

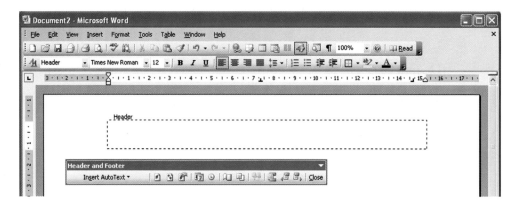

Figure 4.2: The header box

The dotted line will not appear in your document – it just indicates the header area.

You won't need all the buttons in the Header and Footer toolbar for this exercise, but it's useful to know what some of them are for.

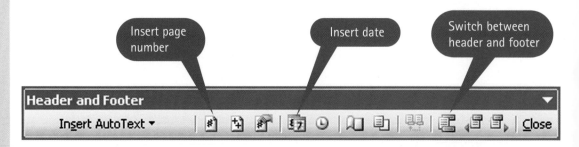

Figure 4.3: The Header and Footer toolbar

You can use the Tab key to tab to the centre or right hand side of the header or footer.

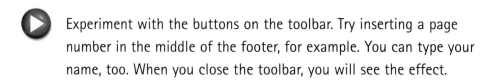 Experiment with the buttons on the toolbar. Try inserting a page number in the middle of the footer, for example. You can type your name, too. When you close the toolbar, you will see the effect.

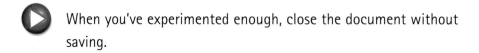 When you've experimented enough, close the document without saving.

 In a new Word document select View, Header and Footer.

Inserting WordArt

You can create the special text effect in the header box using the
WordArt button on the Drawing toolbar.

Click on the WordArt button. ————————————

Choose a text effect from the WordArt Gallery and click OK.

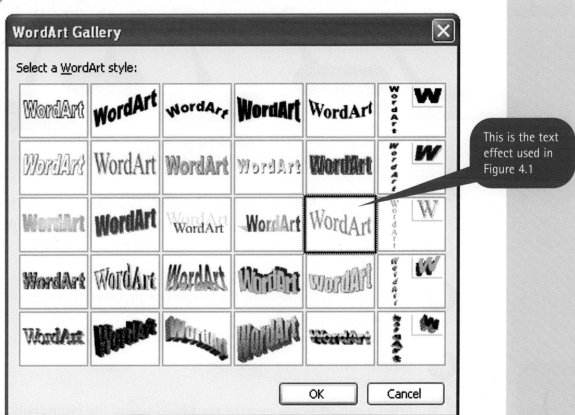

This is the text
effect used in
Figure 4.1

Figure 4.4: The WordArt gallery

Type the words Chess Club into the next dialogue box that appears,
change the font to Comic Sans MS and click OK.

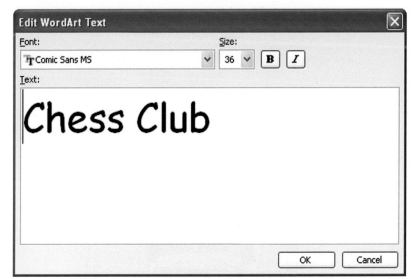

Figure 4.5: Editing the WordArt text

Tip:

Click on the WordArt if the toolbar is not displayed.

The text will be inserted into your document and the WordArt toolbar will be displayed:

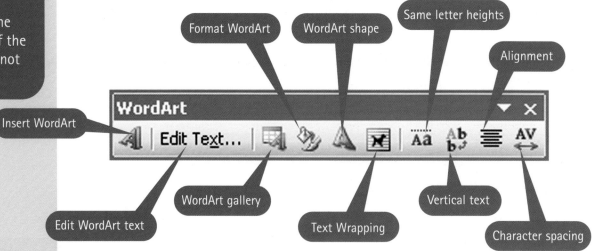

Figure 4.6: The WordArt toolbar

Try out some of the buttons on this toolbar. You can change the shape of the letters, rotate them, make them all the same height... Have fun!

- Insert some blank lines into the header box to make it deep enough to take the WordArt.

- Drag the WordArt into the header box.

- Insert a clip art image into the right hand side of the header box.

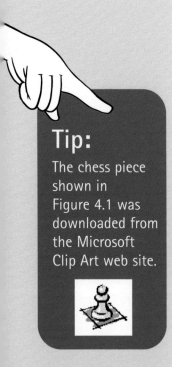

Tip:

The chess piece shown in Figure 4.1 was downloaded from the Microsoft Clip Art web site.

28

Inserting shapes

The four small circles after the WordArt text have been inserted using the Oval tool on the Drawing toolbar.

▶ Click on the Oval tool and draw a small circle (holding your finger on the Shift key will ensure a perfect circle).

▶ Copy and paste this circle so that you have four in a line after the WordArt text. (Hold down Ctrl and Shift while you drag the circle into position.)

▶ Select all four circles by clicking on each one with your finger on the Shift key. Right-click on the circles and select Grouping, Group.

The four circles will now be treated as one object so, for example, you could size them altogether.

▶ Use the Fill tool on the Drawing toolbar to colour the circles in.

▶ Use the Line tool on the Drawing toolbar to draw a line at the bottom of the Header box (keeping your finger on the Shift key ensures a straight line).

▶ Use the Line Color tool on the Drawing toolbar to change the colour of the line.

▶ Click on the Switch Between Header and Footer button on the Header and Footer toolbar (see Figure 4.2).

Inserting a text box

We will add a text box giving details of the School in the Footer box.

▶ Click on the Text Box tool on the Drawing toolbar and draw a text box the same width as the Footer.

▶ Type the school address and centre it as shown in Figure 4.1.

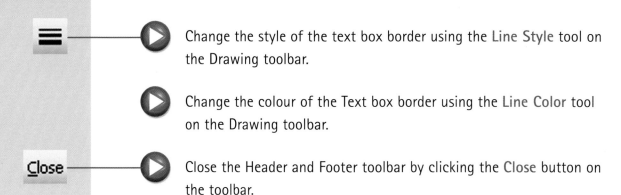

Change the style of the text box border using the Line Style tool on the Drawing toolbar.

Change the colour of the Text box border using the Line Color tool on the Drawing toolbar.

Close

Close the Header and Footer toolbar by clicking the Close button on the toolbar.

Inserting a field

You can insert today's date beneath the header in a special way using a Field.

From the menu select Insert, Field. Then select Date and Time in the Categories box and Date in the Field names box.

Select a date format as shown below and click OK.

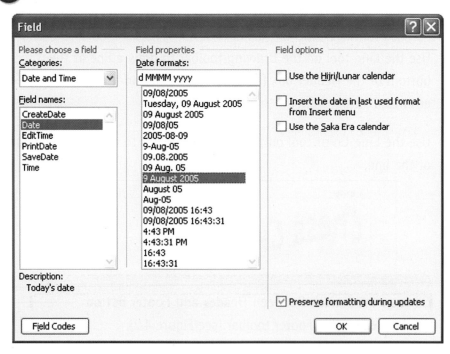

Figure 4.7: Formatting the Date field

Now you can type the rest of the letter as shown in Figure 4.1.

Save the letter as Chess letter.doc.

The letter shown is typed in a standard business format with all paragraphs aligned to the left and one blank line between paragraphs. The letters Enc. at the end of the letter indicate that there is an enclosure (a schedule of matches in this case).

30

Using the same header and footer

You can use the same header and footer for a news bulletin or a newsletter.

▶ Delete the body text of the letter (leaving the header and footer) and type in the text for a news bulletin.

▶ Save this document as Chess news.doc.

▶ Delete the body text of the news bulletin (leaving the header and footer) and type in the text for a newsletter.

▶ Save this document as Chess newsletter.doc.

Saving as a template

Instead of having to keep deleting the contents of the documents we could just save the header and footer as a template which can be opened up time and time again with new data saved each time as a different document.

▶ Open Chess newsletter.doc.

▶ Delete all the newsletter text leaving just the header and footer.

▶ Select File, Save As.

The following dialogue box will be displayed.

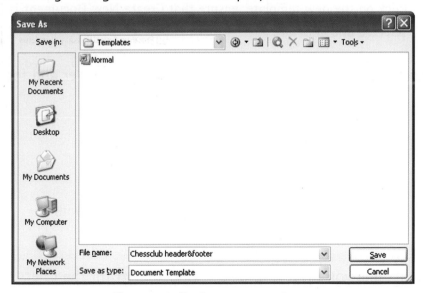

Figure 4.8: Saving as a template

▶ In the File name box type Chessclub header&footer.

 In the Save As type box select the Document Template option.

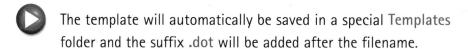 The template will automatically be saved in a special Templates folder and the suffix .dot will be added after the filename.

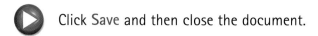 Click Save and then close the document.

Using the template

Select File, New and select Templates, On my computer... (General Templates in Office 2002) in the New Document task pane.

In the dialogue box you should see the name of your new template.

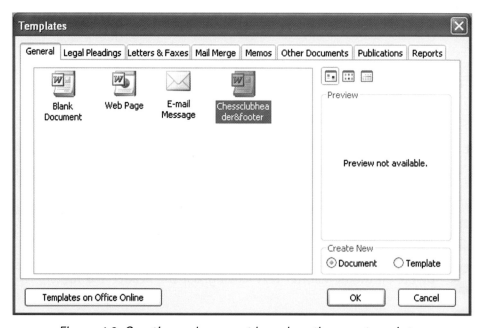

Figure 4.9: Creating a document based on the new template

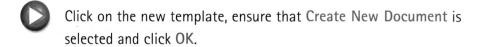 Click on the new template, ensure that Create New Document is selected and click OK.

A new document will open with the Chess Club header and footer.

 Enter some information into the document.

 Select File, Save As.

This time save the document as you normally would, with an appropriate name.

The next time you need to produce a document for the Chess Club, you simply open a new document based on the Chess Club template (i.e. Chessclub header&footer.dot).

Chapter 5

Creating Tickets

In this chapter you'll learn how to design and print tickets, labels or business cards. You can buy special perforated card to print them on, or you can just print your tickets on thin card and then cut it up.

Project: Create tickets for a disco

Your sheet of tickets will look something like this:

Figure 5.1: A sheet of tickets

Setting up the margins

▶ In a new Word document select File, Page Setup.

▶ Measure the margins of your chosen stationery carefully, or use the dimensions shown in Figure 5.2.

Figure 5.2: Setting up the margins

▶ Click the Paper tab, make sure that the paper size is set to A4 and click OK.

▶ Save the blank document as Discotickets.doc.

Setting up the grid

▶ Measure the dimensions of the cards in your chosen stationery. In this example, we will be producing ten cards on the page, each 9cm by 5.1cm.

Draw ▾

▶ Click Draw on the Drawing toolbar and select Grid.

▶ Set the grid dimensions of the tickets as shown in Figure 5.3 and click OK.

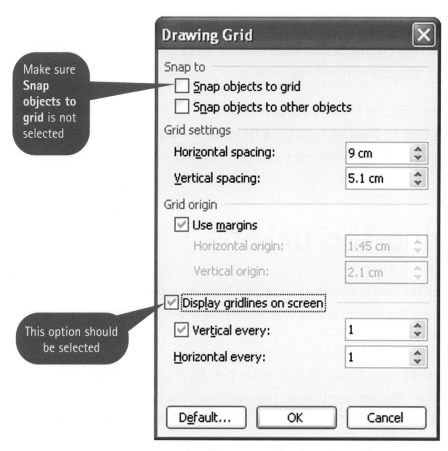

Make sure **Snap objects to grid** is not selected

This option should be selected

Figure 5.3: Setting the grid

Creating the tickets

▶ Use the Text box tool to insert a text box small enough to fit inside ————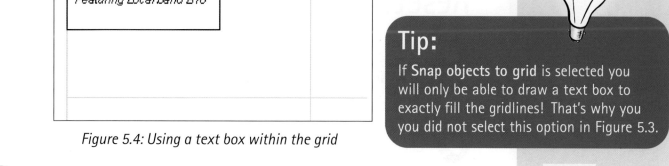
the gridlines and still leave room for the clip art picture.

▶ Type the two lines of text inside the text box as shown below.
(The top line is 16pt Arial, the second line 12pt but you can use
whatever size and colour you like.)

Valentine's Disco

Featuring Local band B18

Figure 5.4: Using a text box within the grid

Tip:
If **Snap objects to grid** is selected you
will only be able to draw a text box to
exactly fill the gridlines! That's why you
you did not select this option in Figure 5.3.

▶ Select the text box and use the Line Color tool to select
No Line.

▶ Now draw a second text box below and put in it the address, date,
time and price. Remove the border of the text box.

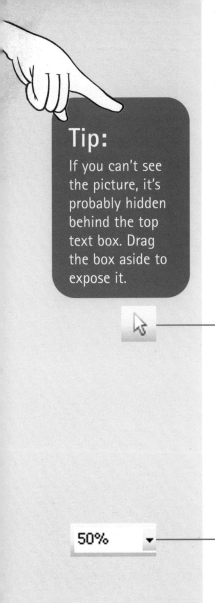

Tip:

If you can't see the picture, it's probably hidden behind the top text box. Drag the box aside to expose it.

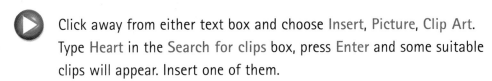
Click away from either text box and choose Insert, Picture, Clip Art. Type Heart in the Search for clips box, press Enter and some suitable clips will appear. Insert one of them.

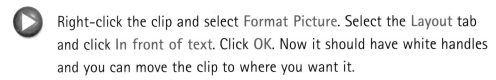
Right-click the clip and select Format Picture. Select the Layout tab and click In front of text. Click OK. Now it should have white handles and you can move the clip to where you want it.

Copying the ticket

Click the Select Objects tool on the Drawing toolbar and draw a box around the entire card so that all objects within the card are selected.

Click the right mouse button inside the ticket and select Grouping, Group. This ensures that all the objects on the card will be treated as a single object.

Select Draw, Grid again and select Snap objects to grid. Click OK.

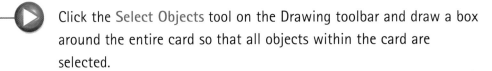
Use the Zoom button to change the view to 50% so you can see most of the sheet.

Keeping the Ctrl key pressed and using the mouse, you can now copy the card 9 times to the rest of the page by dragging it. It will snap into place as soon as you are in the right area. You should end up with a sheet of 10 tickets.

Save your document.

Resetting the grid

Note:

Don't forget to restore the grid and remove the gridlines! If your screen looks like graph paper next time you use it, you forgot!

Before you start working on another document select Draw, Grid again and deselect Snap objects to grid and Display gridlines on screen.

Check that the grid size has been set back to its original settings. This is usually .32cm horizontally and vertically.

Newspaper Columns

Using columns

In Chapter 3 you learned how to arrange information in columns using tabs and tables. Documents such as newsletters, magazines or newspapers use snaking columns which means the information fills the first column and then continues at the top of the second column etc. To show this we will reformat part of a geography project. This file is available for you to download from the Payne-Gallway web site:

www.payne-gallway.co.uk/fws

HISTORY OF ~~AUNWICH~~

 Open the downloaded document rawgeographyproject.doc.

To see text in columns you must be in Print Layout view.

Tip:
You can also change view using the buttons at the bottom left of your screen.

Print Layout view

▶ Select View, Print Layout from the main menu bar.

▶ Go to Page 3 of the document.

▶ Highlight the paragraphs of text under the heading What do we know about its history?

▶ Click the Columns button on the Standard toolbar. Drag across two ———— columns and release the mouse button.

The text is arranged in two columns. You can also have a line between columns or adjust the width between the columns.

▶ Select Format, Columns. The following dialogue box is displayed.

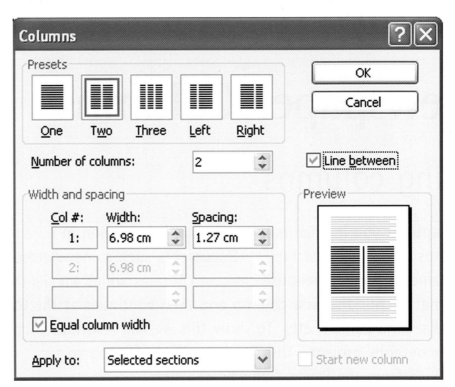

Figure 6.1: Formatting columns

 Check the line between box. Your text should now appear like this:

What do we know about its history?

The first development on the site was probably a Romano-British community, and in Anglo-Saxon days it became the most important commercial centre in East Anglia. Early in the 7th century, when Sigebert became king of East Anglia, Dunwich was chosen as his capital, and a bishopric was founded before 650. The community received a charter from King John (reigned 1199-1216).

Dunwich became a wealthy port, but severe coastal erosion caused its decline. In 1347 more than 400 houses were washed away in a storm, and similar disasters occurred in 1570.

Until 1832, Dunwich returned two members to Parliament in spite of its small population. The corporation was abolished in 1886. The population in 1981 was 129.

Dunwich also figures in literary history. Fitzgerald took Carlyle to visit Dunwich in 1855; Fitzgerald also came to Dunwich whilst he was translating Omar Khayyám in 1859. Jerome K. Jerome spent annual holidays here around 1900 at lodgings provided by a Mrs Scarlet who also kept a shop.

Swinburne's 'By the North Sea' from *Studies in Song* (1880) was inspired by his visit. Edward Thomas finished the first draft of his biography of Richard Jefferies in 1907 in a coastguard cottage at Minsmere, high up on 'a heaving moor of heather and close gorse', half a mile away from where the ruined church had half fallen over the eroded cliff.

Figure 6.2

Justification

At the moment your text is left-aligned. Documents that are formatted into columns often use justified text – this is when the text goes straight down the left and right margins.

 Highlight both columns of text.

 Click the Justify button on the Formatting toolbar. ———————————

What do we know about its history?

The first development on the site was probably a Romano-British community, and in Anglo-Saxon days it became the most important commercial centre in East Anglia. Early in the 7th century, when Sigebert became king of East Anglia, Dunwich was chosen as his capital, and a bishopric was founded before 650. The community received a charter from King John (reigned 1199-1216).

Dunwich became a wealthy port, but severe coastal erosion caused its decline. In 1347 more than 400 houses were washed away in a storm, and similar disasters occurred in 1570.

Until 1832, Dunwich returned two members to Parliament in spite of its small population. The corporation was abolished in 1886. The population in 1981 was 129.

Dunwich also figures in literary history. Fitzgerald took Carlyle to visit Dunwich in 1855; Fitzgerald also came to Dunwich whilst he was translating Omar Khayyám in 1859. Jerome K. Jerome spent annual holidays here around 1900 at lodgings provided by a Mrs Scarlet who also kept a shop.

Swinburne's 'By the North Sea' from *Studies in Song* (1880) was inspired by his visit. Edward Thomas finished the first draft of his biography of Richard Jefferies in 1907 in a coastguard cottage at Minsmere, high up on 'a heaving moor of heather and close gorse', half a mile away from where the ruined church had half fallen over the eroded cliff.

Figure 6.3: Justified columns

Paragraph formatting

The paragraphs would be easier to read if they were spaced out.

 Highlight both columns.

 Select Format, Paragraph.

 In the dialogue box select a First line special indentation and 3pt spacing before the start of a paragraph as shown overleaf.

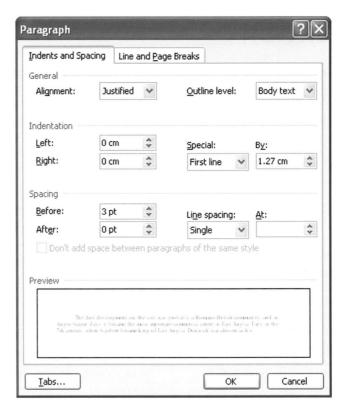

Figure 6.4: Setting paragraph formatting

Your text should now be looking something like this:

What do we know about its history?

The first development on the site was probably a Romano-British community, and in Anglo-Saxon days it became the most important commercial centre in East Anglia. Early in the 7th century, when Sigebert became king of East Anglia, Dunwich was chosen as his capital, and a bishopric was founded before 650. The community received a charter from King John (reigned 1199-1216).

Dunwich became a wealthy port, but severe coastal erosion caused its decline. In 1347 more than 400 houses were washed away in a storm, and similar disasters occurred in 1570.

Until 1832, Dunwich returned two members to Parliament in spite of its small population. The corporation was abolished in 1886. The population in 1981 was 129.

Dunwich also figures in literary history. Fitzgerald took Carlyle to visit Dunwich in 1855; Fitzgerald also came to Dunwich whilst he was translating Omar Khayyám in 1859. Jerome K. Jerome spent annual holidays here around 1900 at lodgings provided by a Mrs Scarlet who also kept a shop.

Swinburne's 'By the North Sea' from *Studies in Song* (1880) was inspired by his visit. Edward Thomas finished the first draft of his biography of Richard Jefferies in 1907 in a coastguard cottage at Minsmere, high up on 'a heaving moor of heather and close gorse', half a mile away from where the ruined church had half fallen over the eroded cliff.

Figure 6.5: Formatting columns

Inserting a picture across columns

In magazines particularly, you often see articles with graphics positioned across the columns. If the graphic has an irregular shape you can make the text wrap to that shape.

▶ Click anywhere within the two columns of text.

▶ Select Insert, Picture, Clip Art and insert an irregular-shaped clip art image.

▶ Click on the picture and you will see that it has black sizing handles around it.

▶ Right-click the picture and select Format Picture.

▶ In the Format Picture dialogue box click the Layout tab.

▶ Click the Tight layout option and then OK.

The sizing handles around the picture should now be white. This means you can drag the picture to the position you require.

▶ Drag the picture to the centre and size it so that it looks something like this:

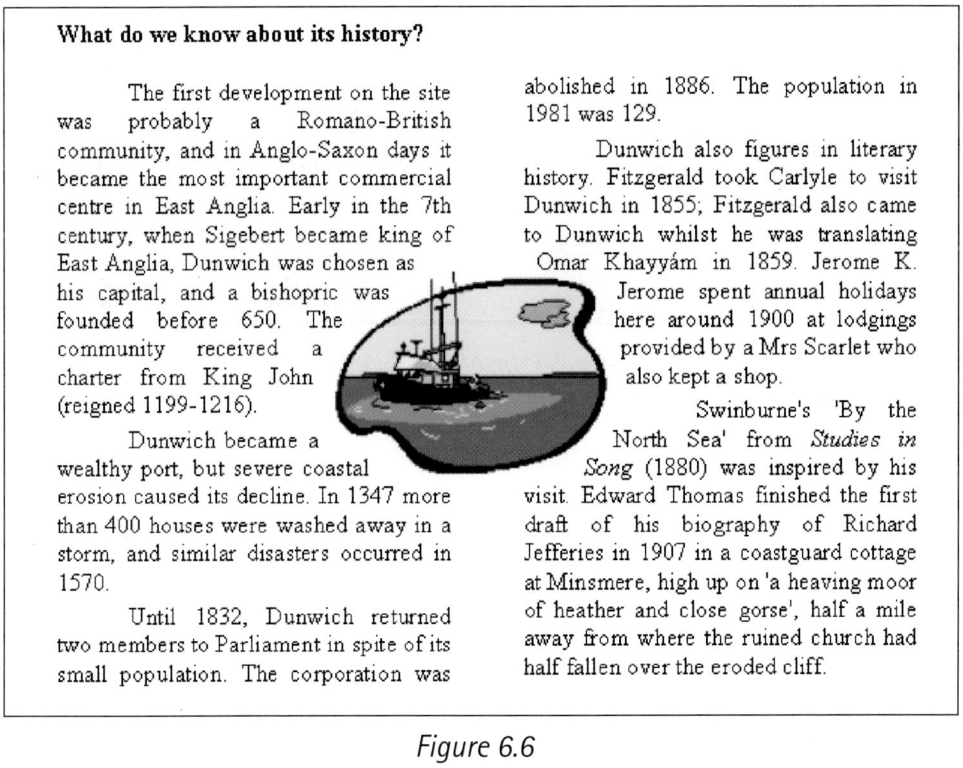

Note:
Select **Format**, **Columns** and remove the line between the columns.

What do we know about its history?

The first development on the site was probably a Romano-British community, and in Anglo-Saxon days it became the most important commercial centre in East Anglia. Early in the 7th century, when Sigebert became king of East Anglia, Dunwich was chosen as his capital, and a bishopric was founded before 650. The community received a charter from King John (reigned 1199-1216).

Dunwich became a wealthy port, but severe coastal erosion caused its decline. In 1347 more than 400 houses were washed away in a storm, and similar disasters occurred in 1570.

Until 1832, Dunwich returned two members to Parliament in spite of its small population. The corporation was abolished in 1886. The population in 1981 was 129.

Dunwich also figures in literary history. Fitzgerald took Carlyle to visit Dunwich in 1855; Fitzgerald also came to Dunwich whilst he was translating Omar Khayyám in 1859. Jerome K. Jerome spent annual holidays here around 1900 at lodgings provided by a Mrs Scarlet who also kept a shop.

Swinburne's 'By the North Sea' from *Studies in Song* (1880) was inspired by his visit. Edward Thomas finished the first draft of his biography of Richard Jefferies in 1907 in a coastguard cottage at Minsmere, high up on 'a heaving moor of heather and close gorse', half a mile away from where the ruined church had half fallen over the eroded cliff.

Figure 6.6

Charts

Adding a chart

A table of data can often be easier to understand if it is shown as a chart.

Go to page 8 of the geography project where you will find a table of data showing the sizes of pebbles found in a sample on the beach.

Highlight the numbers in the table.

Select Insert, Object.

Click on Microsoft Graph Chart and then click OK.

Tip:

If you have created a chart in Microsoft Excel you can easily **Copy** and **Paste** it into your Word document.

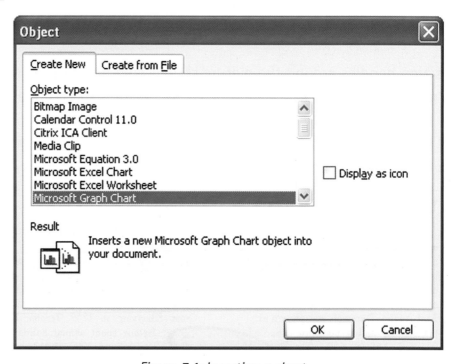

Figure 7.1: Inserting a chart

You should see the following:

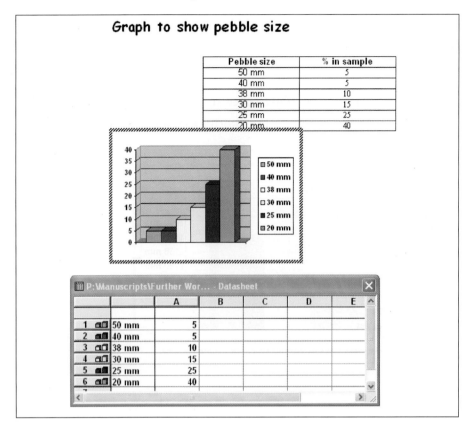

Figure 7.2

A datasheet and a chart have automatically been produced for you.

▶ Close the datasheet by clicking the Close icon in the top right of its
window.

▶ Drag one of the corner black handles around the new chart to make
it larger.

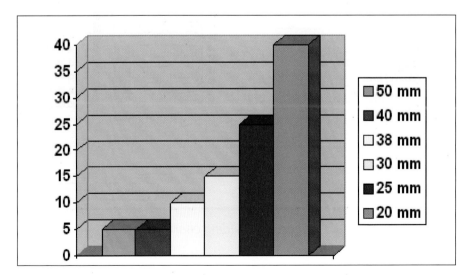

Figure 7.3

Formatting the chart

▶ Double-click the chart.

▶ Right click within the white space to the right of the X-axis and select Chart Options from the shortcut menu.

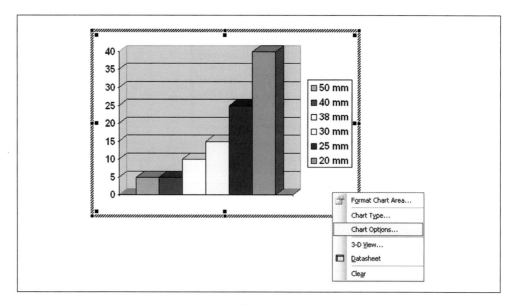

Figure 7.4

▶ In the Chart Options dialogue box click the Titles tab and enter any missing titles as shown.

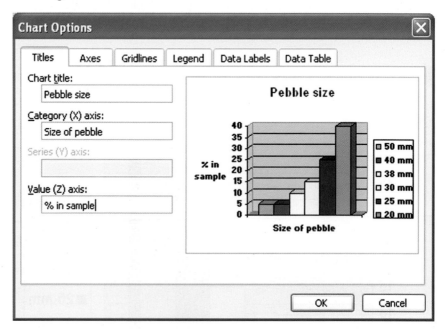

Figure 7.5: Adding chart titles

▶ Try changing the style of gridlines and moving the legend using the other options in this dialogue box.

Right-click the chart again and this time select Format Chart Area.

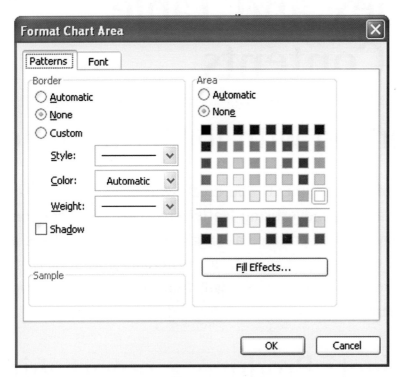

Figure 7.6

This dialogue box allows you to add a coloured border, change the colour of the chart background and change the style of text used in the chart.

If you right-click an individual bar in the chart and select Format Data Series you can change the colour and shape of that bar.

Experiment!

Tip:
Try right-clicking the chart and selecting **Chart Type**. You can then choose to display the data as a pie chart.

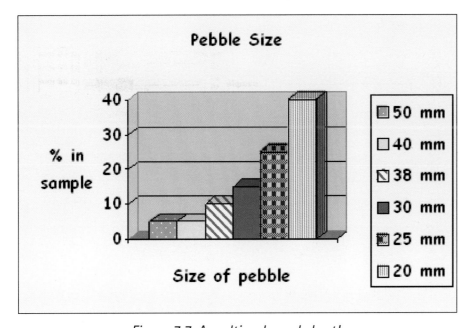

Figure 7.7: A multi-coloured chart!

Index and Table of Contents

Working with longer documents

Many of the documents you create will be fairly short – a letter, a timetable, an advertising leaflet etc. However occasionally you may need to produce a longer document – perhaps a school project or a business report. In this chapter we look at features of Microsoft Word that you will find useful for these types of document.

Project: Produce a report with an index and table of contents

This project requires a long document to work with. The one used here is the geography project and is available for you to download from the Payne-Gallway web site:

www.payne-gallway.co.uk/fws

You could adapt the instructions for one of your own projects or reports.

Tip:
To download the file, type the web site address into your web browser (e.g. Internet Explorer) and follow the instructions given on the web page

Numbering pages

 Open the downloaded document rawgeographyproject.doc.

 From the Insert menu select Page Numbers.

In the Page Numbers dialogue box choose the settings as shown below.

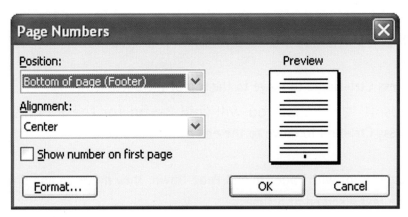

Figure 8.1: Specifying page numbers

 Click OK, then click the Print Preview button on the Standard toolbar. ———————

 Click the Multiple Pages button on the Print Preview toolbar and ——————— drag over the icons to display four pages at once.

You should see the page numbers at the bottom of each page except the title page. You can click on a page number to zoom in on it. There is no number on the first page because in the dialogue box you chose not to have one.

 Click Close on the Print Preview toolbar.

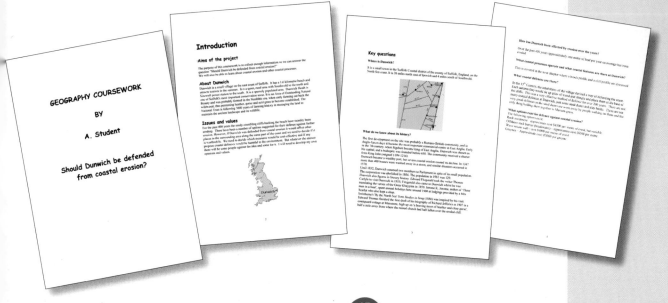

Moving around a long document

There are lots of ways to move around your document – dozens, probably, and very few people know them all. You just need to learn the way you find quickest and easiest and stick to it.

- Find the Ctrl key on the keyboard, down in the left-hand corner. It's a useful key, always used in combination with another key.

- Now find the keys marked Home, End, Page Up, Page Down.

- Press Ctrl-Home to move to the top of the document.

- Press Ctrl-End to move to the end of the document.

- Experiment with Page Up and Page Down. They move up and down the text a screen at a time.

- Find out what Home and End do when you don't have the Ctrl key pressed. (You'll find they move the cursor to the beginning and end of the current line.)

- Find the arrow keys which are in a little block under the Home and End keys you have just been using.

- Experiment with these – they move the cursor left or right one character at a time, or up and down one line at a time.

- If you select Edit, Find and enter a word you are looking for in a document, you will be taken straight to that word (try F5 as a shortcut too).

Tip:

"Press **Ctrl-Home**" means hold down the **Ctrl** key with one finger while you press the **Home** key with another finger.

Creating a table of contents

If you scroll through the document and highlight some of the headings you will find that styles have been applied to them to maintain a consistent format (Chapter 2 explains how to set up styles).

The easiest way to create a table of contents is to use these defined styles.

 Click at the end of the last line on the title page. Press Ctrl-Enter to insert a blank page.

 Type a heading Contents. Press Enter twice.

 From the Insert menu select Reference, Index and Tables and then click the Table of Contents tab.

The following dialogue box will be displayed.

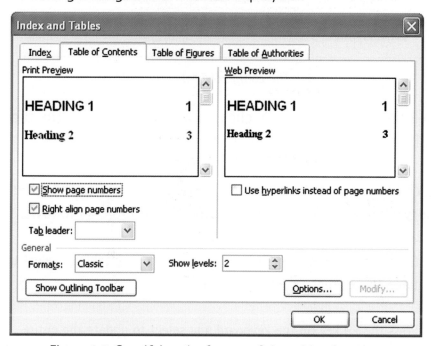

Figure 8.2: Specifying the format of the table of contents

 Select the options as shown above, with 2 in the Show levels box.

We have selected a classic format that will list the two main heading types together with leader dots and right-aligned page numbers. You can experiment with the different options and choose a format you think most suitable for your document.

 Click OK.

Tip:

Another way to insert a blank page is to select **Insert, Break** and then click **Page Break, OK**.

Tip:

In 2000, select **Insert, Index and Tables** and click the **Table of Contents** tab.

The table of contents should be displayed on page 2.

Figure 8.3: The completed table of contents

You will find that if you ctrl+ click on a page number in the table you will be taken automatically to that part of the document.

If you change one of the headings in the document or the page numbers change then you need to update the table as follows.

 Click in the left margin beside the first line of the table to select the table. (It's enough to select one line.)

 Press the F9 key on the keyboard and select to update the entire table.

Tip:
Your TOC (Table of Contents) may not appear shaded.

Tip:
To return to the TOC again, click the back arrow on the Web toolbar.

Creating an index

An index lists in alphabetical order the topics or important words in a project or book, along with the pages they appear on. It appears at the end of a document.

We will create some sample index entries for the geography project.

Marking the entries

To create an index, you must first mark the index entries in your document.

▶ Open the document rawgeographyproject.doc if it is not already open.

▶ Select the first word or phrase you want in the index, for example the word Sizewell in the second paragraph of the introduction.

▶ Press Alt-Shift-X on the keyboard.

The dialogue box shown in Figure 8.4 will be displayed.

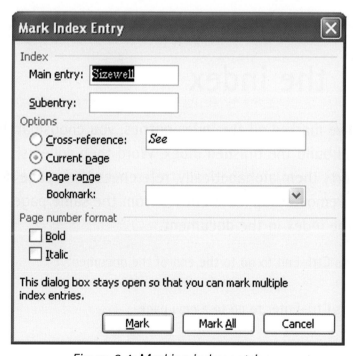

Figure 8.4: Marking index entries

 Click on Mark All.

This will mark every occurrence of the word Sizewell in the document.

Formatting characters will appear in the text as in Figure 8.5.

About ·Dunwich¶
Dunwich·is·a·small·village·on·the·east·coast·of·Suffolk.··It·has·a·beach·and·attracts·
tourists·in·the·summer.··It·is·a·quiet,·rural·area·with·Southwold·to·the·north·and·Sizewell·{·
XE·"Sizewell"·}·power·station·to·the·south.··It·is·a·sparsely·populated·area.··¶

·¶

Issues ·and ·values¶
▪ If··Dunwich··was·defended·from·coastal·erosion·it·would·affect·other·places·in·the·

Figure 8.5: Formatting characters

 Click Close.

 Highlight the phrase coastal defences in the middle of the next paragraph.

 Press Alt-Shift-X on the keyboard, click Mark All and then Close.

Tip:
You can keep the Mark Index Entry dialogue box open.

You would normally work through the whole document marking any new entries. We will create the index with just these two entries. Before you do this, you must hide the formatting characters again as they take up space and may change the page numbers in the index!

 Click the Show/Hide button on the Standard toolbar.

Build the index

After you've marked all the index entries, you choose an index design and build the finished index. Word then collects the index entries, sorts them alphabetically, references their page numbers, finds and removes duplicate entries from the same page, and displays the index in the document.

 Press Ctrl-End to go to the end of the document.

 Press Ctrl-Enter to go to a new page.

 Type the heading Index in Heading 1 style and press Enter twice.

 Select Insert, Reference, Index and Tables.

 Click the Index tab.

Tip:
In Word 2000 select Insert, Index and Tables.

The following dialogue box will be displayed.

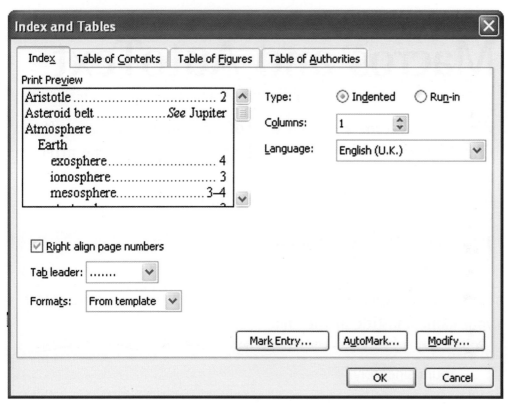

Figure 8.6: Creating the index

 Select the options as shown in Figure 8.6 and click OK.

The index should be displayed and look something like this.

Index

coastal defences...3, 5
Sizewell 3, 14

Figure 8.7: The index so far

If you add, delete, move, or edit index entries or other text in a document, you should manually update the index. For example, if you edit an index entry and move it to a different page, you need to make sure that the index reflects the revised entry and page number. To manually update the index:

 Click in the left margin near the top of the index to select it.

 Press F9 on the keyboard.

Try adding some more index entries and updating the index!
Then save your work.

Chapter 9

Macros and AutoText

When you become a regular user of word processing you often find that there are tasks that you are carrying out time after time. This can be frustrating and inefficient – you need to learn some ways to automate these tasks.

Using AutoText

For example, every time you write a letter you may want to insert your name and title at the end.

Yours sincerely

Henry Davidson
Senior Editor
Education Department

Figure 9.1

AutoText is text which is inserted for you automatically. Word comes with a number of built-in AutoText entries, such as salutations and closings for letters.

 In a new Word document select Insert, AutoText and choose an AutoText entry from the Closing category.

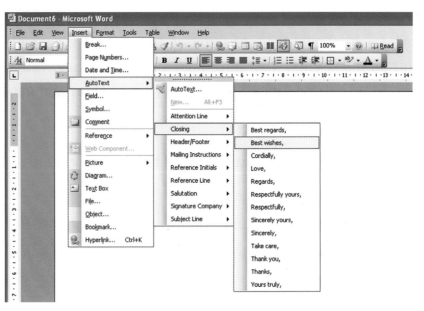

Figure 9.2

You can also create your own AutoText entries.

 Select Insert, AutoText, AutoText and type in your new entry.

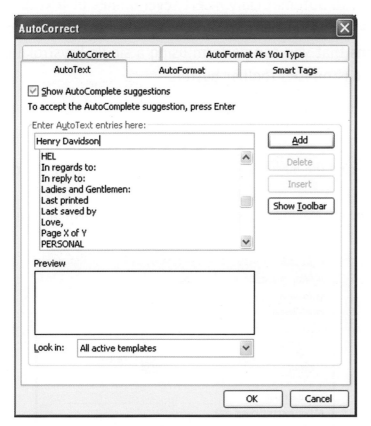

Figure 9.3

 Click Add and then click OK.

You can now use your AutoText entry in the same way as you did the built-in entry above, but this time your entries (one line at a time) will be in the Normal category.

Recording a macro

If you want to automatically insert several lines of text in one go, a macro will be a quicker option. A macro is a series of recorded instructions that you can perform using a single keystroke or by clicking a customised toolbar button.

Tip:

Macro names must begin with a letter and cannot contain spaces.

▶ Open a new document.

▶ To record the macro, select Tools, Macro, Record New Macro.

▶ Name the macro and type in a description as shown in Figure 9.4. Click OK.

Figure 9.4

Every keystroke you perform from now on will be recorded as part of the macro.

▶ Enter the text as shown in Figure 9.1.

▶ Stop the macro by clicking the Stop Recording button on the Stop Recording toolbar.

Figure 9.5

Running the macro

▶ Move to a new line in your Word document.

▶ Select Tools, Macro, Macros.

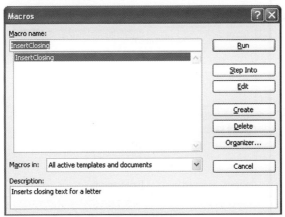

Figure 9.6

▶ Click on your macro name (InsertClosing) and then click the Run button.

The closing text for your letter should be entered.

Assigning a macro to a key combination

It can be even quicker to run a macro if you assign it to a keyboard shortcut. Perhaps you need to add a disclaimer to certain documents that you send out to customers. Let's record a macro to insert the text and run the macro by pressing Alt+D on the keyboard.

▶ In a new Word document select Tools, Macro, Record New Macro.

▶ Name the macro Disclaimer and enter a description.

Figure 9.7

 Click the Keyboard icon.

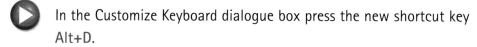 In the Customize Keyboard dialogue box press the new shortcut key Alt+D.

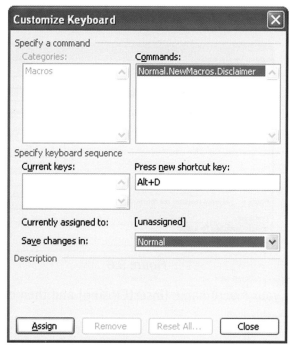

Figure 9.8

 Click Assign and then click Close.

 Now record the macro by typing in your disclaimer notice:

 Click the Stop Recording button.

 Move to a new line in your Word document and press Alt+D on the keyboard to run your macro.

Assigning a macro to a toolbar button

Instead of pressing Alt+D to run the macro to insert the disclaimer notice we can create a customised button that will run the macro when clicked.

▶ Select Tools, Macro, Record New Macro.

▶ In the Record Macro dialogue box (Figure 9.7) name the macro Disclaimer2, click the Toolbars icon and the Commands tab.

Figure 9.9

▶ Drag the entry out of the Commands box and onto one of your toolbars.

Figure 9.10

▶ With the Customize window still open, right-click the new button again. Type in a new name Disclaimer2.

Figure 9.11

▶ Click Close in the Customize dialogue box and record your macro. Then try out your new button!

Tip:

You can add a symbol to the button if you like, using **Change Button Image**.

Mail Merge

Ever received a letter like this?

"Dear **Mr Wilson**

You, **Mr Wilson** of **Ipswich** could soon be holding a cheque for £10,000,000!!! Just send for our catalogue…"

A letter like this is produced using a mail merge. Mail merge can also be used to produce labels or to print directly onto envelopes.

Project: Produce personalised letters for a Junior Chess League

Remember the letter you created in Chapter 4? Suppose you need to send the same letter to ten schools taking part in the championship. You will also need to print address labels for the envelopes.

Creating the letters

There are four basic steps involved in setting up a mail merge:

Step 1:   Open or create the letter (called the main document).

Step 2:   Open or create the list of names and addresses (called the data source).

Step 3:   Insert the merge fields in the main document.

Step 4:   Merge the data source with the main document.

Step 1

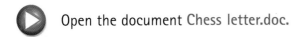 Open the document Chess letter.doc.

On the Tools menu click Letters and Mailings, Mail Merge Wizard.
(Word 2000: Mail Merge.)

You will see one of the following:

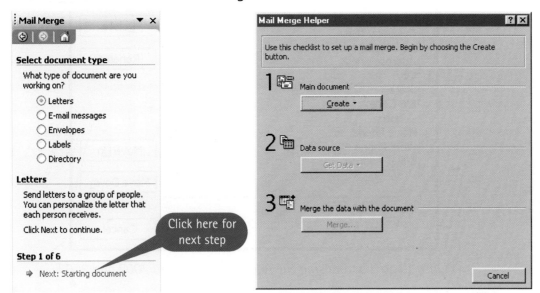

*Figure 10.1: The Mail Merge task pane (2002/2003)
and Mail Merge Helper (2000)*

Word 2002 and 2003: with Letters selected click Next, then Next again.
Word 2000: click Create, Form Letters then Active Window.

Step 2

Word 2002 and 2003: select Type a new list then click Next.
Word 2000: in the Mail Merge Helper dialogue box, click Get Data
then Create Data Source.

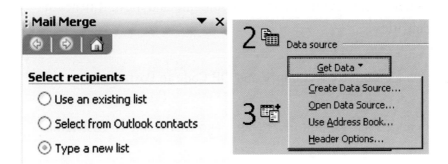

Figure 10.2: Specifying where to get the data from in 2002/2003 (left) and 2000

Specifying the fields in Word 2002 and 2003:

(Word 2000 see next page.)

▶ In the New Address List window, click the Customize button.

Figure 10.3a: Customising the Address list in Word 2002 and 2003

▶ Select the field name Company Name and then click Delete.

▶ Repeat this for City, State, Home Phone, Work Phone and E-mail Address. (Leave ZIP Code and Country.)

▶ Click Add, type in a new field that we would like to add, JobTitle, and click OK.

▶ Move this data field in the list by clicking the Move buttons until it is beneath Last Name.

▶ Add another new field name Schoolname and move it beneath JobTitle.

▶ Change Country to **County** and ZIP Code to PostalCode.

▶ Change First Name to FirstName and Last Name to LastName.

▶ Click OK then Close. You will be asked to save this data source, so locate the folder you want to put it in and save it as ChessContacts.

Tip:
Use the **Rename** button.

Now go to **Entering data.**

62

Specifying the fields in Word 2000:

The following dialogue box will be displayed:

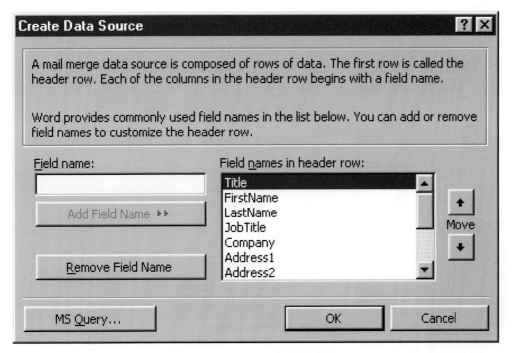

Figure 10.3b: Specifying the field names in Word 2000

This allows you to specify which data fields you want to include in the data source.

▶ Click the field name Company and then click Remove Field Name.

▶ Repeat this for City, State, Country, HomePhone and WorkPhone. (Leave PostalCode.)

▶ In the Field name box, type in the name of a new field that we would like to add, Schoolname.

▶ Click Add Field Name.

▶ Move this data field up the list by clicking on the upward arrow button until it is beneath JobTitle.

▶ Add another new field name County, move it up the list beneath Address2 and click OK.

▶ You will be asked to save this data source, so locate the folder you want to save it in and save it as ChessContacts.

Entering data

In 2000 click **Edit Data Source** at the next prompt.

 In Word 2002 and 2003, click the Edit button in the Mail Merge Recipients window.

A form will be displayed in which you can enter the details about the people who are to receive the letter.

 Fill in the fields as in Figure 10.4. (Word 2000 is very similar.)

Add
County: Suffolk
Postal Code: RB61 6NM

It doesn't matter if one or more address lines are blank.

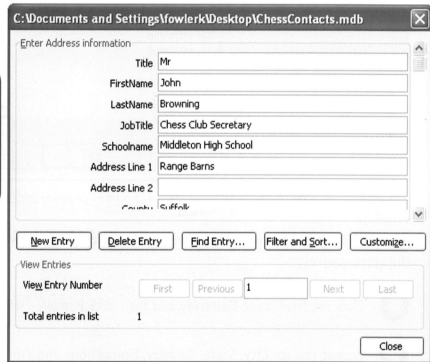

Figure 10.4: Entering the names and addresses

 When you have completed the details click New Entry.

You will be presented with a blank form (don't panic, the information you have just typed in will have been saved automatically).

Word 2000 Add New.

 Make up details of five more Chess Club secretaries at different schools and enter their details as above or use the names and addresses shown in Figure 10.11.

Word 2000 OK.

 Click Close when you have entered the details of all the people.

 In Word 2002 and 2003 show the Mail Merge toolbar. (Right-click on a toolbar and select it from the list.)

Step 3

You should now have the main document on the screen.

▶ Highlight the text Mr John Browning.

▶ Click the Insert Merge Field button on the Mail Merge toolbar. ———————

in 2002
and 2003

The merge fields appear in a new window or, in Word 2000, on a droplist below the button.

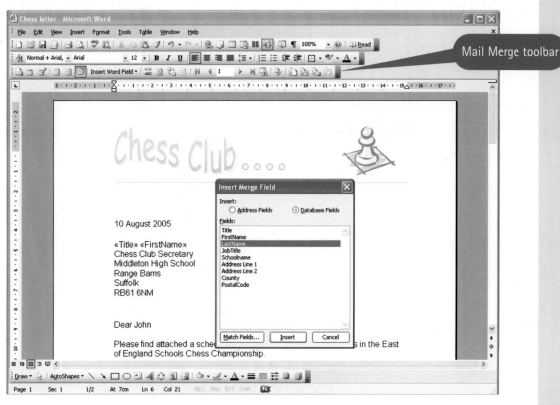

Figure 10.5: Inserting merge fields

▶ Click Title.

▶ In Word 2002 and 2003 click Insert, then Close.

▶ Press the space bar.

▶ Click the Insert Merge Field button.

▶ Enter First Name and Last Name in the same way.

In Word 2002/2003 if you press the space bar in the Insert Merge Field window this may insert an extra field, but you can delete it later!

▶ Highlight the Job title Chess Club Secretary.

▶ Click Insert Merge Field.

▶ Click JobTitle. (In Word 2002 and 2003 click Insert, then Close.)

▶ Repeat for the fields Schoolname, Address Line 1, Address Line 2, County, PostalCode and for FirstName in the salutation line.

The letter should look something like this:

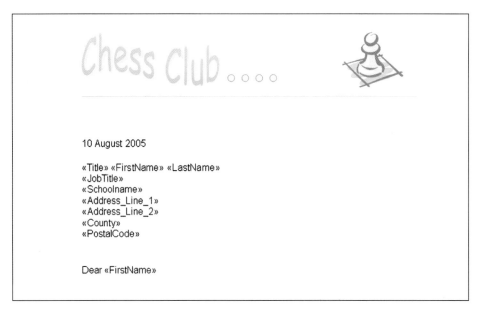

Figure 10.6: The letter with the Insert Merge Fields shown

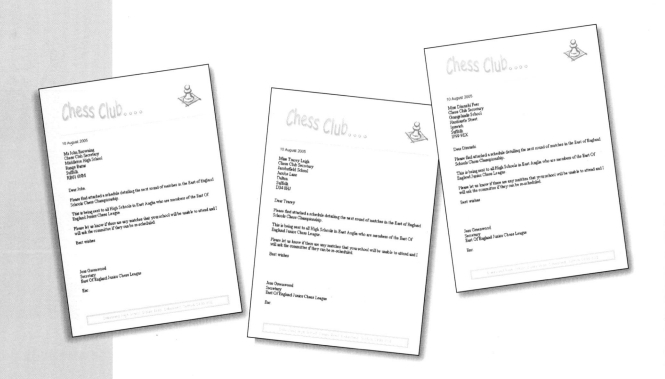

Step 4

▶ Click the Merge to New Document toolbar button. ────────────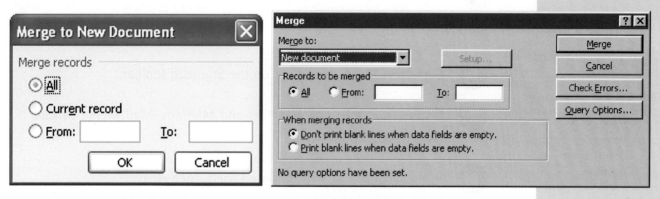
   Word 2000: Click Tools, Mail Merge, Merge.

▶ In the following dialogue box click OK or Merge.

Figure 10.7: Merging the files: Word 2002 and 2003 (left) and 2000

Your form letters will be displayed in a new file called Letters 1 or
Form Letters 1.

▶ Scroll through the document to see all six letters.

▶ Save the file and then print the letters as usual.

Creating mailing labels

Now for the labels to stick on the envelopes. You can use the same name and address data stored in ChessContacts and choose to create labels instead of Form Letters this time. Once again there are four steps.

Step 1

▷ Click New Blank Document on the Standard toolbar.

▷ On the Tools menu click Letters and Mailings, Mail Merge Wizard (Word 2000: Mail Merge).

▷ In the Mail Merge pane choose Labels, then Next.
Word 2000: Under Main Document click Create, Mailing Labels, then Active Window.

Step 2

▷ Click the Open Data Source button on the Mail Merge toolbar.
Word 2000: In the Mail Merge Helper box under Data Source, click Get Data then Open Data Source.

▷ Select the file ChessContacts and click Open.

▷ Click Next.
(Word 2000: click on Set Up Main Document.)

Step 3

The following dialogue box appears (similar in Word 2000) which requires you to enter the details of the labels you will be printing on.

Tip:
If the type of label you want to use is not listed in the Product number box, you might be able to use one of the other listed labels or you can create your own custom labels by clicking on **New Label** and entering the specifications.

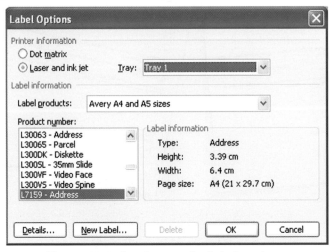

Figure 10.8: Setting up the label options

Select a type of label and click OK.

Word 2002 and 2003

A page of labels appears with the insertion point in the first, ready to insert the merge fields.

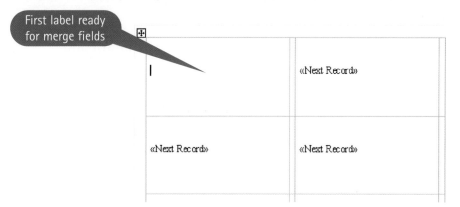

First label ready for merge fields

Figure 10.9: The label document in Word 2003

 Click the Insert Merge Field button on the Mail Merge toolbar.

 Double-click Title, FirstName, LastName, then click Close.

 Insert spaces between the fields, then press Enter at the end to start a new line.

 Keep entering fields until you have entered the whole address.

Word 2000

 In the next dialogue box click Insert Merge Field and click the Title field.

 Press the space bar then insert FirstName in the same way.

 Press the space bar again, then insert LastName.

 Press Enter to go to the next line. Keep entering fields until you have entered the whole address, then press OK.

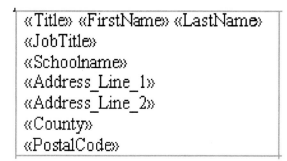

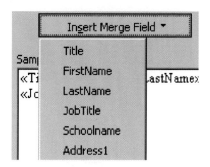

Figure 10.10: Choosing the fields for the labels:
Word 2002 and 2003 (left) and 2000

Note:
Every other label has a <<Next Record>> field.

Step 4

▶ Click the Merge to New Document toolbar button.
Word 2000: Click Tools, Mail Merge, Merge.

▶ Click OK in the dialogue box shown in Figure 10.7.

A document displaying the fields will have been automatically created. Look for it on the task bar – with a name like Labels1 or Document 3 etc.

▶ Save this document as Labelfields.

Your actual labels with the names and addresses will be displayed in a new document Labels2.doc.

▶ Save and print the labels with the label stationery loaded in the printer.

Mr John Browning Chess Club Secretary Middleton High School Range Barns Suffolk RB61 6NM	Miss Tracey Leigh Chess Club Secretary Jacobsfield School Jacobs Lane Dalton Suffolk D34 8HJ	Miss Dimushi Feer Chess Club Secretary Grangelands School Hardcastle Street Ipswich Suffolk IP99 9ZX
Mr Sharif Dasre Chess Club Secretary Field Lane Comprehensive Field Lane Destry Norfolk G67 9KL	Miss Ann James Chess Club Secretary Maine High School Lees Lane Great Halford Essex I78 9HJ	Mr Nigel Smith Chess Club Secretary Ockwell High School St James Road Ockwell Norfolk G45 7YH

Figure 10.11: The printed labels

A conditional merge

It is also possible to select specific data records to merge by choosing selection criteria (or "rules").

Suppose you have met the Suffolk chess club secretaries and given them their letters already. So now you only want to print labels for the schools not in Suffolk.

▶ Make sure you have the document Labelfields open.

▶ In Word 2002 and 2003, click the Mail Merge Recipients button and in the dialogue click Edit then Filter and Sort.

▶ In Word 2000, choose Tools, Mail Merge and in the Mail Merge Helper click Query Options.

Select the **Filter Records** tab.

Figure 10.12: Selecting the records for the mail merge

▶ Select County from the Field drop-down box.

▶ Select Not equal to in the Comparison box.

▶ Type Suffolk in the Compare to box.

▶ Click OK. (In Word 2002 and 2003 close the other dialogue windows.)

▶ Click the Merge to New Document toolbar button.
Word 2000: Click Tools, Mail Merge, Merge.

The labels for non-Suffolk schools only should be displayed (3 in total).

▶ Save and print this file with your label stationery loaded in the printer.

Graphics

There are two basic types of graphics that you can use in Microsoft Word documents: drawing objects and pictures.

You have already used several drawing objects in previous chapters including AutoShapes, lines, WordArt and text boxes. You can use the Drawing toolbar to change and enhance these objects with colours, patterns, borders, and other effects. They are referred to as Vector Graphics and can be stretched, scaled and resized without distortion. Because a high degree of accuracy can be achieved with this type of graphic they are often used for technical drawings and Computer-Aided Design (CAD) applications.

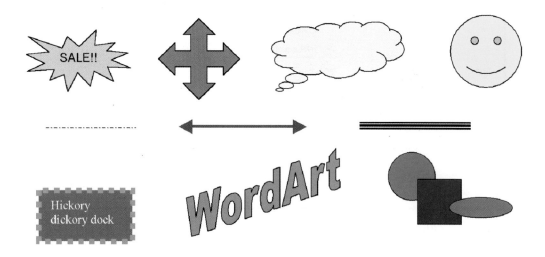

Figure 11.1: Examples of vector graphics created in Word

Pictures and photographs downloaded from the Internet, retrieved from a CD-ROM, captured with a digital camera or a scanner, and clip art are saved in a different way from vector graphics. File formats include .bmp, .jpg, .gif, and .tif (these suffixes are added to the filename automatically when the file is saved). You can insert these files into your Word documents and then change and enhance the pictures by using the options on the Picture toolbar and a limited number of options on the Drawing toolbar. These pictures are referred to as Bitmap Graphics.

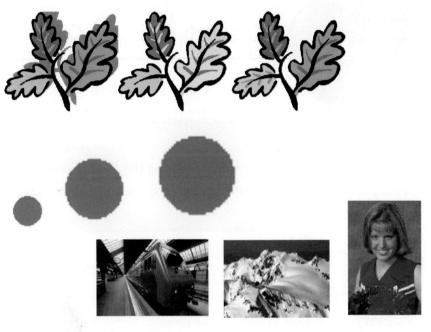

Figure 11.2: Some examples of bitmap graphics

Bitmap images can be created in a painting package such as Windows Paint. To edit this type of image in greater detail a software package such as Adobe PhotoShop or Jasc Paint Shop Pro is required.

The advantage of bitmap images is that individual pixels can be changed, allowing detailed editing. However, problems can arise when sizing a bitmap image – if you increase the size you see unsightly white spaces and jagged edges as shown by the red circles in Figure 11.2.

Project: Use vector graphics to produce a logo for a drinks company

The logo will look like this.

Ipswich Original Cola

Figure 11.3: The completed logo

 In a new Word document draw a circle using the Oval tool on the Drawing toolbar. Keeping your finger on the Shift key as you drag will make a perfect circle.

 Fill the circle in black using the Fill tool.

 Inside the circle draw a rectangle for the letter i using the Rectangle tool. (It will be vertical at this point.)

 Draw a circle for the dot and fill it in yellow.

 Draw a text box using the Text box tool and type in it the letter C in Times New Roman font, bold style, 48pt size and yellow.

 Fill the text box in black and position it appropriately in the black circle.

 Draw a red circle and place a smaller black circle over the top.

 Group the two circles together by selecting them both (keep your finger on the Shift key) and right-clicking. Select Grouping, Group. Move these into position in the black circle so that they are slightly overlapping the other two characters.

▶ Using the Line tool, draw a line across the black circle extending on —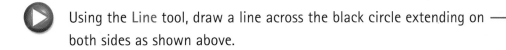
both sides as shown above.

▶ Make the line 1.5pt using the Line Style tool.

▶ Send the line behind the black circle by selecting it and then clicking
Draw from the Drawing toolbar. Then select Order, Send to Back.
(Or, you can right-click and select Order, Send to Back).

▶ Draw a text box above the line on the right-hand side and type the
name of the product in Comic Sans MS font, 18pt size.

▶ Delete the line around the text box using the Line Color tool and —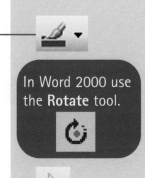
selecting No Line.

In Word 2000 use
the **Rotate** tool.

▶ Finally rotate the letter i slightly by clicking the rectangle. Drag the
green circle at the top of the shape clockwise a little and the shape
should tilt to the right. Move the yellow dot above it.

▶ Use the Select Objects tool to drag around the complete logo to —
select all the different parts. Right-click on one of the objects and
select Grouping, Group.

▶ Save your logo as IOCLogo.

We will be using it in the next exercise.

Enhancing pictures

There are some features on the Picture toolbar that allow you to make simple enhancements to pictures.

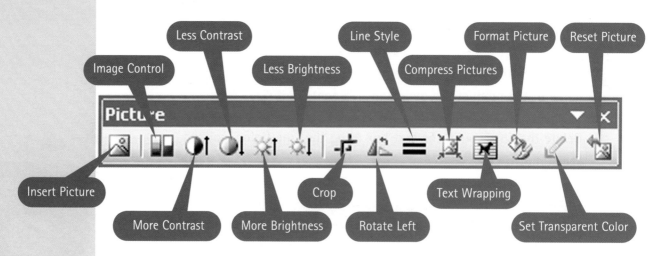

Figure 11.4: The Picture toolbar

Experiment with some of these features before you move on to the next project.

▶ In a new Word document insert a clip art image.

▶ With the image selected try increasing and decreasing the contrast and brightness. Change it to grayscale using the Grayscale option on the Image Control button and crop part of the image away.

Project: Design an advertisement for a new product

Many documents combine both vector and bitmap graphics.
We will produce an advertisement for Ipswich Original Cola that incorporates clip art, photographs, text and autoshapes.
The completed advert should look something like this:

Figure 11.5: The completed advert

The photographs that have been used can be downloaded from the Payne-Gallway web site www.payne-gallway.co.uk/fws.

Or, you could use your own pictures! You will need several to create your advertisement, so make sure you know where they are saved.

Creating the advertisement

▶ In a new word document set each margin to 1.5cm and the page to landscape orientation.

▶ Create the main heading in WordArt. Use the WordArt toolbar to create special effects.

▶ Underneath this draw a text box and enter the text And join the stars!!

▶ Change the font of this text to 14pt, Arial and delete the border of the text box by setting the line colour to No Line.

▶ Insert the picture Rocketlaunch.jpg. Size and position it as shown in Figure 11.5.

▶ Insert the clip art image of the man drinking the cola – this was found on the Microsoft Design Gallery Live web site. (Try typing drinking in the Search box.) Size and position him over the rocket.

▶ Draw some autoshape stars, some large and some small.

▶ Fill the small stars in yellow.

▶ To insert the pictures in the larger stars, select a star and click the Fill Color tool followed by Fill Effects.

▶ Select the Picture tab.

The following dialogue will be displayed:

AutoShapes ▾

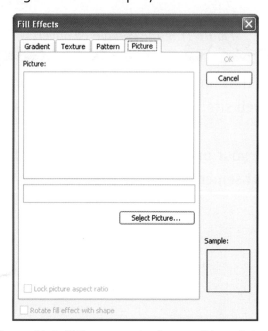

Figure 11.6: Filling an autoshape with a picture

▶ Click on Select Picture and go to the folder in which you saved your pictures. Click on the filename and then click OK.

▶ Click OK in the Fill Effects dialogue box and the picture will be inserted into the star autoshape.

▶ Repeat for the other large stars using the files in the folder Stars at www.payne-gallway.co.uk/fws or files of your own.

▶ Draw a rectangle around the advert and fill in light grey.

▶ Copy and paste the logo you created earlier into the bottom right-hand corner.

▶ Draw a text box on the right-hand side of the advert, slightly overlapping the main photograph and enter the text as shown.

▶ Remove the text box border and fill it in the same light grey as before.

That's it – your advert can now go to press and sales should rocket!

Index